Bonnie Nagy

The beauty in nature we behold is like the greatest music to our ears.

South Park, Colorado

Bernie and Linda Nagy

Credits and Acknowledgments:

Authors: Bernie and Linda Nagy
Photography: Bernie Nagy
Executive Editor: Tom Locke
Associate Editors: Linda Nagy, G. & M. Wilmoth
Botanical Review: Steve Yarbrough, Botany (MA)
Fungi Review: Beth Rognerud, Mycologist
Cover Design: Bernie and Linda Nagy
Art and page design: Bernie and Linda Nagy
Color separations: High Country Artworks LLC
Copyright 2012   High Country Artworks LLC

Special thanks to Gary Nichols for providing us with that special South Park color map.

Published by:
High Country Artworks LLC, P.O. Box 1795, Fairplay, Colorado 80440
Visit us online at: www.HighCountryArtworks.com
Printed and bound in China

First Edition, Second in Series, January 2012
ISBN: 978-0-9840636-8-0
Library of Congress Control Number: 2011909661

Cover: Wildflowers, wildlife, and mountains become symbols of South Park.
Title Page: A butterfly and bumblebee share a coneflower.

High Country Artworks LLC
P.O. Box 1795
Fairplay, Colorado 80440
Website and ordering information:
www.SouthParkBook.com
Email: info@HighCountryArtworks.com

"The winds will blow their own freshness into you, and the storms their energy, while cares will drop away from you like the leaves of Autumn." -John Muir

Above: In fall, a journey along County Road 107 off Colorado Highway 9 offers unstoppable color splendor with aspens lining the road. *Facing page:* The evening sun blazes through a twisted pine atop a hiking trail at Eleven Mile State Park.

*"The sun does not shine for a few trees and flowers,
but for the wide world's joy."* -Henry Ward Beecher

South Park is a high grassland basin located right in the center of Colorado. It lies near the headwaters of the South Platte River and is surrounded by a ring of mountain ridges and peaks. The Mosquito Range to the northwest has 25 peaks more than 13,000 feet high and five peaks over 14,000 feet. With its diversity of terrain, South Park is abundant with wildlife and wildflowers.

In 2009, through federal legislation, South Park was designated a National Heritage Area. With many historical structures, geological wonders, and flora and fauna that are distinct to the region, South Park is recognized as one of only 49 National Heritage Areas in the United States.

All of the wildflowers in this book were photographed in South Park and are shown in their natural settings in the vicinity as indicated. Every attempt was made to accurately describe the flowers, but this book should not be considered a botanical reference; there are numerous other such sources available in print.

South Park is ever-changing. Each season has its own beauty and charm. Every return to an area reveals new insights. From late spring into the summer wildflower season, on through the magnificent golden fall foliage, and into the solitude of a Rocky Mountain winter, South Park teases and delights everyone with the splendor of the ever-changing seasons.

About the Authors

Bernie and Linda Nagy at their South Park home with a view toward South Park's Mosquito Range.

Bernie Nagy grew up in the Austrian Alps, where he studied graphic arts, printing and photography. Many of his early photos and stories were published during his high school years. He has photographed images throughout Europe, the Middle East, Mexico, South America, New Zealand, Australia and North America and has had photo essays and travelogues published by newspapers and magazines.

In 1967 he emigrated to the United States, where he met his wife, Linda, and became a naturalized citizen in 1973. Bernie completed his studies with the New York School of Photography and was a member of the Atlanta Press Photographers Association.

Linda Nagy, born in Atlanta, Georgia, attended the University of Georgia and received BFA and MFA degrees in graphic design. Her career began at Hallmark Cards, where she designed greeting cards. She returned to Georgia and established a retail and direct marketing business with Bernie.

Linda is a member of Women of Watercolor in Colorado and enjoys plein air painting and teaching newcomers painting and sketching. Bernie and Linda Nagy share their passion for South Park. When they moved to Fairplay, Colorado, the couple was so impressed with the beauty surrounding their new residence that Bernie began documenting the area with photographs.

He and Linda often traveled to remote locations that could only be reached by hiking or by four-wheel-drive vehicle to take photographs of South Park at different times of the year.

The result was Bernie's first book, <u>Colorado's South Park, High Country Paradise.</u> In 2010, the book received several awards, including "Best International Regional Travel Essay Book" at the 2010 New York International Book Fair.

The first book whetted Bernie and Linda's appetite for more. They felt as if the South Park story and beauty could not be contained in one volume. Therefore, they set out again to capture images of the ever-changing scenery throughout the seasons and also more of South Park's wildflowers, many of which are rare.

"Again, this second book is a labor of love, and I hope it inspires others to go out in nature and discover the beauty and bounty that South Park delivers year-round. If you photograph nature and wildflowers, please remember, no photograph is worth damaging your subject or the fragile environment," Bernie said.

Besides photography and graphic arts, Bernie and Linda also enjoy hiking, four-wheel drives, winter sports and worldwide travel.

"How glorious the greeting the sun gives the mountains!"
-John Muir

The mountains and a lone windmill contrast with a blazing sunrise along U S 24 near Hartsel.

Dedication:

This book is dedicated to our children, Christina and Markus, and our son-in-law, Charles, who are all outstanding photographers, and to our budding photographer, our granddaughter, Amari.

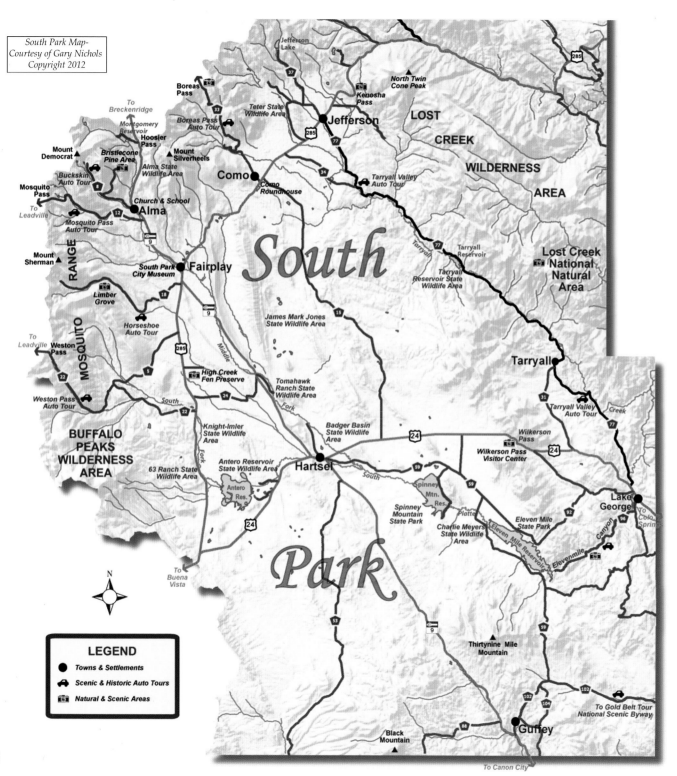

South Park Map-
Courtesy of Gary Nichols
Copyright 2012

LEGEND
- ● Towns & Settlements
- 🚗 Scenic & Historic Auto Tours
- 📷 Natural & Scenic Areas

Facts about South Park, Colorado

The scenic beauty of South Park includes prairies, fertile grassy plains, reservoirs, small rivers, and gentle hills surrounded by high mountain ridges.

Area: Approximately 1,000 square miles around the headwaters of the South Platte River including surrounding mountain ridges, make up South Park.

Elevation: The elevation varies from 8,500 to 10,000 feet, but surrounding peaks soar to more than 14,000 feet above sea level.

Population: Approximately 8,000.

Towns and Communities: Fairplay, Alma, Como, Jefferson, Hartsel, and in the greater South Park area, Guffey and Lake George.

County seat: The town of Fairplay.

Mountains: The Mosquito Range has 25 peaks over 13,000 feet and five peaks over 14,000 feet, including mounts Lincoln, Cameron, Bross, Democrat and Sherman. The Park Range, from Kenosha Pass and Red Cone to Mt. Silverheels and to Hoosier Pass, forms the northern rim of South Park. Smaller mountains include Buffalo Peaks, the Front Range, Kenosha Mountains, Black Mountain, Thirtynine Mile Mountain, Puma Hills and the Tarryall Mountains.

Reservoirs: Antero, Eleven Mile, Tarryall, Spinney Mountain and Montgomery.

Mining: Gold was discovered in 1859 on Tarryall Creek. The Fairplay-Alma area produced an estimated $250 million in gold, silver and other minerals until 1949. The highest silver mines operated just below the summits of Mt. Lincoln and Mt. Bross.

Tourism: South Park attracts more than three million visitors a year.

Fairplay Attraction: South Park City Museum

Additional information on South Park: See links on the website www.SouthParkBook.com

A view from the Loveland mountain meadows shows Pennsylvania Mountain in the background.

Contents

Early summer warms the plains and the high country, but snow and ice melt slowly in the upper mountain region around Emma Lake. Soon, the first flowers will appear, such as Marsh Marigolds, Globeflowers, Alpine Buttercups and Alpine Sunflowers that face the east to welcome the rising sun.

8

Spring, A New Awakening

The Pasqueflower has stringy leaves and fine hairs that help insulate it against the cold. Also called Prairie Crocus, it is one of the earliest plants to bloom in the high country.

Top: White Marsh Marigold appear soon after snow melt in early summer. *Bottom left:* Globeflowers, with rounded petals and lobed leaves, grow in marshy, subalpine meadows. *Bottom right:* Snow Buttercups spring up through the melting snow along a mountain lake.

Top left: Alpine Forget-Me-Nots and Moss Campion share the tundra in the high meadows from early June through August. *Bottom left:* Tiny white Alpine Phlox form a carpet of blooms among the rocks.

Above: Snow still covers the high country, but warmer weather encourages a break from winter captivity for a hike on a late spring day. In upper mountain meadows or along a creek, there just might be pussy willows to greet winter-starved eyes.

Receding snow at Boreas Pass

Lingering snow forms interesting patterns on a hillside near the summit
of Boreas Pass. Billowing clouds foretell late spring showers.

Springtime Aspens

Quaking Aspens in profusion reach tall into the sky along
Forest Road 107. Only a few show hints of spring growth.

"I decided that if I could paint that flower in a huge scale, you could not ignore its beauty."
-Georgia O'Keeffe

A single Wild Iris is silhouetted against a bubbling brook glistening in the early summer sun. *Facing page:* From June through mid-July, Irises populate a field along U.S. 285 near Red Hill Pass and transform it into a sea of blue.

Top left: Locoweed can be white or purplish and is toxic for animals and humans. *Top center:* The tiny Pgymy Bitterroot is often found soon after snow melt. *Bottom left:* The Tufted Evening-Primrose blooms in late spring and throughout the summer. *Bottom center:* Tiny Wild Candytuft can be found in late spring in alpine meadows. *Right:* A Mountain Dryad growing among rocks is surrounded by Alpine Sandwort blossoms with their moss-like leaves.

16

At Camp Como, forest openings and meadows are filled with an array of wildflowers in late spring. Clusters of Wild Roses, Nodding Sunflowers and Locoweed are just a few of the many varieties to delight the senses. *Inset:* The Wood's Rose is both lovely and fragrant.

Above: The Clark's Nutcracker inhabits conifer forests at timberline. Its long bill and black tail feathers help to distinguish it from the Gray Jay. *Right:* Limber pines survive harsh winds, extreme elements and lightning strikes and seem to defy death. Their turns and knotholes are evidence of their struggles throughout the centuries.

"Of all man's works of art, a cathedral is greatest. A vast and majestic tree is greater than that."
-Henry Ward Beecher

An ancient limber pine lives despite its stripped arched trunk. It has stiff needles in bundles of five without the resin spots that the bristlecone pine needles have. Exposed trunks form twisted art sculptures at the 11,000-foot-high grove along the northern slope of Sheep Mountain.

"If you would know strength and patience, welcome the company of trees."
-Hal Borland

Limber pines take root among the lichen-covered rocks and spread their crowns skyward.

"For in the true nature of things, if we rightly consider, every green tree is far more glorious than if it were made of gold and silver." -**Martin Luther**

High above the Valley of the Sun subdivision and Sacramento Creek, the morning sun tints the clouds pink. Due to the rough alpine environment and high winds, a twisted bristlecone pine grows almost parallel to the ground.

Summer, Time to Explore

Left: The Rocky Mountain Columbine, also known as the Colorado Blue Columbine, is Colorado's state flower and can be found on higher moist slopes and in aspen groves.

Top right: Steller's Jays are bold and noisy. These handsome birds use their crests to communicate.

Among Rocky Mountain Columbines and Blue Lupines, clusters of Mountain Death-Camas with waxy six-petal flowers grow up to three feet tall in mountainous rocky fields and forests.

Top left: Orange Sneezeweed may cause sinus irritation for some humans.
Top center: The Rosy Paintbrush grows on rocky slopes in alpine heights.
Top right: The Alpine Sunflower is also called Old-Man-of-the-Mountain.

Bottom left: Firecracker Penstemon has tubular flowers and blooms from June to September. *Bottom center:* The fragrant Wallflower has four-petaled blossoms in clusters.
Bottom right: Sticky Geranium flowers can be found in clumps in sunny forest openings.

24

On top of Mount Silverheels or at the meadows of Black Powder Pass (shown above), one can see Old-Man-of-the-Mountain wildflowers, also called Alpine Sunflowers, which always face east.

25

Top left: Lousewort flowers look like curved bird's beaks. *Top center:* Delicate Alplilies bloom in alpine meadows in the summer. *Bottom left:* Wild White Geraniums with fine pink veins grow in clusters in forest openings. *Bottom center:* Wooly Actinea or Stemless Hymenoxys has grey-green leaves covered with fine hairs. *Far Right:* The pink to reddish-purple Elephantella are shaped like tiny elephants' heads with trunks and ears. *Opposite page:* Summertime wildflowers add color to Buckskin Gulch.

"Trees are poems that earth writes upon the sky. We fell them down and turn them into paper, that we may record our emptiness." - Kahlil Gibran

This single leaning bristlecone pine tree at Windy Ridge
is perhaps the most photographed one in Colorado.

"The tree is a slow, enduring force straining to win the sky."
-Antoine de Saint-Exupery

The remains of an old bristlecone pine tree at Beaver Ridge still stand as a testament to its struggles over centuries.

Left: A scene from the Bristlecone Pine Scenic Area at Windy Ridge offers views from the ancient forest toward the upper ridges of Mount Bross. *Above:* The bristlecone pine has shiny resin dots on its needles.

A small grove of bristlecone pine trees shades a path at the Bristlecone Pine Scenic Area at Windy Ridge.

Top left: Purple-blue Larkspurs grow along creek beds and in moist meadows.
Top center: Parry's Clover blooms amid Mountain Parsely. *Top right:* The delicate cup-shaped Mariposa Lily is found in the upper meadows of mountain ridges.

Bottom left: Low-growing Penstemon and Field Mouse-Ear Chickweed bloom by roadsides. *Bottom center:* Yellow Heartleaf Arnica is seen from June through August. *Bottom right:* Tiny Blue Mountain Violets bloom in clusters close to the ground.

Above: A close-up of Heartleaf Bittercress shows its four-petaled pure white blossoms. *Left:* Near the top of Boreas Pass, a trickling brook flows below the gravel road with tall Heartleaf Bittercress covering its banks. 33

Wildflowers in bloom

Top left: Mountain Bluebells bloom from mid-June to August along streams and in wet meadows.
Top center: The rare and endangered Wood Lily can be found in moist aspen groves. *Bottom left:* The
Yellow Pea or Golden Banner is an early blooming flower and grows in large clumps.

Bottom center: Yarrow (white) blooms coincidentally with Cinquefoil.
Both are medicinal plants and are used to stop bleeding. *Right:* Purple
Fringe can be found in the high meadows throughout the summer.

"Hope is like a harebell trembling from its birth, ..." -**Christina G. Rossetti**

Above: Around Kite Lake and in the meadows on Loveland Mountain, large fields of Mountain Harebells sway back and forth in the constant winds from the peaks across the Mosquito Range. They can be identified by their five lavender-blue petals forming a bell-shaped blossom. 35

Below the steep slopes of Mount Democrat, Kite Lake glistens in the early morning sun.

Wildflowers, such as white Bistort, pink Dwarf Clover (*top right*), red King's Crown and Yellow Paintbrush (*bottom right*), can be found along Kite Lake. Columbine and Indian Paintbrushes color the banks along a brook at Buckskin Gulch (facing page).

Left: The Sky Pilot is sometimes known as Skunkweed as its emits a strong odor. *Center:* Alpine Thistle and Rosy Indian Paintbrushes flourish in high meadows along the Mosquito Range. *Right:* The one-sided, tall Penstemon grows in clusters in sandy soil.

Facing page: Loveland Mountain offers a view of Buckskin Gulch, below, surrounded by snow-powdered fourteeners. In front, the Frosty Ball Thistle can grow over two feet tall.

Top left: Lupine blooms on clustered spikes and has leaves divided into five to nine leaflets.
Top center: The common Mullein grows into a tall stalk with many small yellow flowers.
Bottom left: Jacob's Ladder grows in the shade around bushes and trees.

Bottom center: Short-growing, Twisted Gentians vary in color, from pink to dark purple. *Above:* Monument Plants, also called Green Gentians, can be spotted along the upper meadows of South Park's mountain ranges.

The tall Miner's Candle (left) blooms in early summer on gravelly foothills. Low-growing Leafy Cinquefoil (top center) and Black-Eyed Susans (bottom center) are seen at Tarryall Creek. Wild Bergamot (top right) and up to six-foot tall Coneflowers (bottom right) are found near roadsides. (Photos by Linda Nagy)

From the lush summer meadow at Beaver Ridge, one sees a grand panoramic view toward the northwest. In the distance are Montgomery Reservoir, Quandary Peak in Summit County, and the road up to Hoosier Pass to the right.

Left: Prairie Smoke or Old Man's Whiskers, grows in front of Shrubby Cinquefoil that covers vast areas at Beaver Ridge meadows below Mount Silverheels. *Above:* A closeup shows the beauty of a single blossom called Prairie Smoke, because it has the look of a puff of smoke.

"If there is magic on this planet, it is contained in water."
-Loren Eiseley

Numerous waterfalls are found throughout the mountains surrounding South Park's grasslands. Chiming Bells and Rosy Paintbrushes (above left) and Rose Crown (at right), grow frequently along the brooks and streams.

Left: Several large waterfalls cascade from upper Mosquito Gulch. In July, the banks along the creeks are covered with large colorful clusters of wildflowers. *Right:* A tall waterfall can be seen from Forest Road 856, a steep and rocky four-wheel-drive trail that cuts through wildflower meadows between Mosquito Peak and Mount Buckskin.

Left: In summer, receding snowfields keep plenty of water streaming down from the high mountains above into Mosquito Gulch. Fireweed grows beside waterfalls.
Right: The rocky drive up to the 13,186-foot-high Mosquito Pass is busy with four-wheel-drive vehicles maneuvering the treacherous curves during the summer.

Left: At the midway point up to Mosquito Pass is the remaining structure of the North London Mine, a symbol of the past mining era. Growing in the meadow are white Bistort, Rose Crown, and purple Elephantella. *Right:* Even in summer, as seen here above Sacramento Gulch, one can encounter patches of fresh snow at higher altitudes along Mosquito Pass Road.

Roadside flowers near Guffey

Above: Adding color to the valley, bright yellow Goldeneyes line both sides of a winding county road near Guffey. The inset photo shows a close-up of the flowers.

To the delight of many travelers, the roadside between Fairplay and Hartsel is covered in midsummer with wide expanses of Blue Flax.

Top left: Red Elderberries look inviting, but can be toxic. *Top right:* In front of the poisonous Amanita muscaria or Fly Agaric, a yellow Senecio is growing.

Bottom left: The Sarcodon imbricatus, or Scaly Tooth Urchin, has dark brown to black raised scales. *Bottom right:* A Clitocybe gibba or Funnel Cap, resembles a bird bath.

Toward the end of Forest Road 431, a large cluster of Butter-and-Eggs, also called Yellow Toadflax, glows in the early morning sun. This is a state-listed noxious weed.

One can find a wide array of wildflowers and rocks of many different colors while hiking along the colorful rolling meadows below West Buffalo Peak, which was an active volcano 28 million years ago. Shown here are the Fringed Gentian (top left), Golden Aster (top center), Mountain Gentian (bottom left), and Blue Penstemon with buzzing bee (right).

52

"Do not follow where the path may lead. Go instead where there is no path and leave a trail." -Ralph Waldo Emerson

From a rocky outcrop at the upper Buffalo Peaks Wilderness, there is a view of a dense fir forest below and toward the southeastern part of South Park in the distance.

An oncoming vehicle creates a dust cloud on County Road 53 near
Hartsel as it seems to escape the looming afternoon thunderstorm.

"When I admire the wonder of a sunset...my soul expands in worship of the Creator."- **Mahatma Gandhi**

A glorious sunset lights the Buffalo Peaks in purplish red to the west of the South Fork of the South Platte River near Hartsel. Rabbitbrush appears in the foreground.

Parry's Primrose patches appear along the banks of a bubbling brook below Mount Silverheels. (Photos by Linda Nagy)

Lost Creek

Left: Slender Blue Penstemons are backlit by the sun in a meadow off County Road 56 at Lost Creek. (Photo by Linda Nagy) *Above:* The delicate Skyrocket, or Fairy Trumpet, survives in sunny, dry forest openings and meadows.

Tarryall

The ever-changing midsummer scenery throughout the Tarryall Valley includes majestic rock formations, lush ranchland, shrubs, and patches of wildflowers.

Right: Pioneers settled in Tarryall in the early 1800s and turned the valley into fertile pasture land. Historic rancher cabins along the winding Tarryall River can be seen from the road. *Top left:* Cut-leaf Daisies break through hard-crusted ground. *Bottom left:* Fringed Sage glows in the sun. (Photos by Linda Nagy)

Water birds

Above left: Water fowl are abundant at all of South Park's reservoirs. Shown are a Canada Goose, a Snowy Egret and Ibises. *Above right:* Gulls bask in the sun. *Bottom left:* An Ibis and an American Avocet search for food. *Bottom right:* A pelican, cormorant and gull pose at Eleven Mile State Park.

Hiking at Eleven Mile State Park

Above: Eleven Mile State Park offers spectacular vistas from all its hiking trails.
Inset: Rabbitbrush stands out along the shoreline of Eleven Mile Reservoir.

Top left: The Bottle Gentian can be found along the many trails at Eleven Mile State Park.

Top center: The purple Musk Thistle (invasive, noxious) grows along lake shores and old fields.

Top right: The bee-attracting Chokecherry shrub has red to black berries.

Bottom left: Hooker's Evening Primrose, like others of the species, opens in the late afternoon and then closes and dies the next morning.

Bottom right: Foxtail Barley fills open areas along Eleven Mile Reservoir's shoreline.

Facing page: Trees and rugged rocks are mirrored in the reservoir along a hiking trail in the state park, while an early morning fog rises in the distance.

The remains of an old settler's cabin on FR 107 are adorned with flowers and grasses on top of what was the roof years ago (above). The Wavyleaf Thistle (top right) and the Rocky Mountain Bee Plant (bottom right) can be found along roadsides.

Wildflower medley

A single blue Skypilot and a yellow Mountain Parsley squeeze through a cluster of deep red Indian Paintbrushes.

Left: Large bushes with rosehips grow along the scenic Elevenmile Canyon Road. *Top right:* Along the river, a Boulder Raspberry blossom, with perfect petals, catches the eye. *Bottom right:* Canada geese enjoy the warmth of the midday sun atop a river-worn rock in the South Platte River.

Along many South Park trails, an array of wildflowers, such as Cutleaf Evening Primrose (top left), Wild Cosmos (bottom left), False Forget-Me-Not (top center), Common Dandelion (bottom center), and Aspen Daisy (right), bloom throughout the summer.

South Park's own beautiful little canyon lies near Guffey. Known locally as Guffey Gorge, it is easily accessible from County Road 102. A short walk, through a meadow and along cliff bottoms, leads to a waterfall and swimming hole. This secret place, known to locals, is definitely worth a visit and a picnic.

Thirtynine Mile Mountain

A spectacular view of South Park, as seen from the meadows of Forest Road 256 in the Thirtynine Mile Mountain area, includes Spinney Reservoir, the Puma Hills, and in the far distance, the Tarryall Mountains.

Autumn, The Golden Season

Left: "Fall Aspens," a watercolor by Author/Artist Linda Nagy, captures the season through another art form. *Above:* The morning sun spotlights an elk with its handsome, velvety rack.

Above: From green to gold, changing aspen leaves indicate that fall is just around the corner. *Right:* The tips of tall, mature aspens show first fall color along Forest Road 254 at Thirtynine Mile Mountain.

Leavick Tarn

Left: On a crisp fall morning, the sun casts a reddish glow on sedges and other ground cover around the Leavick Tarn below Horseshoe Mountain. The still water reflects the mighty mountain behind it.

Top Right: Elephantella, Bistort and Rose Crown share the moist meadows around the base of Horseshoe Mountain. *Bottom Right:* The stems of the Rose Crown (shown), as well as the King's Crown, turn completely red in fall.

Red Hill Pass

Fall is a short but beautiful season in the high country. It is the time to go on a hike or travel by car and relish the brilliant colors throughout South Park. Colors from yellows, to oranges, to deep reds can be seen in September at the ridges of Red Hill Pass along U.S. 285.

Top left: By late August, one can see glimpses of fall at Tumbling Creek along Forest Road 442. *Bottom left*: An old horse buggy contrasts with glimmering aspen leaves. *Right*: Early-morning frost covers the tall grasses beside County Road 22. In the background is a view of the winding road toward Weston Pass.

A grand view from a hillside at the Meyer Ranch shows fall foliage with Buffalo Peaks in the distance.

Elusive moose are making a welcome comeback in South Park. These handsome
specimens were spotted between the willows on South Park's mountain meadows.

Fall comes to Mosquito Gulch. The remains of the historic London Mill are surrounded by colorful willows and shrubs.

Twelvemile Lake

Above left: Along the shoreline of Twelvemile Lake, one can see touches of fall color by late August.
Top right: Sulphur Flowers bloom late into early fall and vary in color from pale yellow to pink and
red. *Bottom right:* The Arctic Gentian is one of the last wildflowers to bloom in late fall.

The scenic Twelvemile Lake, at 11,000 feet, is a short and easy hike from the trailhead off the four-wheel-drive Forest Road 173.

Top left: It looks as if Bonnie and Clyde were here (photo by Linda Nagy). *Top right:* The remnants of a tree struck by lightning give an impression of Pinocchio with his long nose. *Bottom left:* A gutted tree forms an eerie and ghostly mask. *Bottom right:* This weathered tree trunk resembles an elephant's head and trunk.

A dramatic view toward the west reveals a thunderstorm boiling up in the Mosquito Range. *Inset:* An arrastra, a carved-out boulder used for pulverizing ore to separate out precious gold more than a century ago, is surrounded by golden willow leaves along Buckskin Creek.

81

Indian Hills

A hand-hewn fence in the Indian Mountain subdivision helps frame a vista toward the Continental Divide.

Jefferson Lake

Mid-September is a great time to catch fall foliage along the scenic trail that winds around Jefferson Lake.

Left: A Monkshood towers above the grasses and shrubs. *Top center:* Fringed Gentian blooms from July to September.
Top right: The Hoary Willow is one of the many rare plants in the High Creek Fen. *Bottom center:* Few-Flowered Shooting
Stars appear as miniature fireworks displays. *Bottom right:* Shrubby Cinquefoil adds a golden glow to the Fen.

A bleached old spruce tree, surrounded by thriving flora, keeps watch over its beloved home, High Creek Fen. The Fen is a spring-fed wetland, rich in calcium carbonate that supports a large number of rare plants.

Left: From a hillside near County Road 22, one can see the aspen meadows that surround Sheep Valley.
Right: An old settler's cabin along County Road 107 stands behind a small pond mirroring puffy clouds.

"Winter is an etching, spring a watercolor, summer an oil painting and autumn a mosaic of them all." - Stanley Horowitz

Driving in early September with a high-clearance vehicle on Forest Road 261 up to Dicks Peak yields the rewards of an outstanding view. Far in the distance are the Collegiate Peaks in Chaffee County.

"Autumn is a second spring when every leaf is a flower."
-**Albert Camus**

Fall comes to Fairplay

Opposite page and above: September is a colorful time in South Park. Glorious aspen groves surround Fairplay, and it is a perfect time to explore the town, South Park City, the Fairplay Beach Recreation Area and its surroundings.

Along the steep and winding Forest Road 437, a small outcrop of ancient bristlecone pines overlooks Placer Valley and Beaver Ridge.

Left: The crystal clear Montgomery Reservoir lies below the rock glacier walls of Mt. Lincoln.
Right: Around the 12,000-foot-high Wheeler Lake, wildflowers bloom well into September.

Opposite page: The open meadows along Forest Road 433 show grand fall colors beneath the East Buffalo Peak area. *Right:* A rancher rides with his dogs along an aspen-bordered trail.

93

Left: The midday sun shines a filtered light through a canopy of young trees and makes the aspen leaves shimmer along County Road 107 near Black Mountain in the Guffey area.
Below: Dew drops bead on the waxy surface of a golden leaf fallen to the ground.

Above: An aspen leaf covers the dark open wound in a tree's trunk and seems to make a fashion statement from Mother Nature. *Right:* Is this Christmas in September? Aspen leaves, settling on a small pine tree, decorate the boughs like glowing ornaments in the midday sun along a Kenosha Pass forest trail.

A valley and mountain, with layers of fall colors, make a perfect picture opportunity
for the many visitors driving along Boreas Pass Road in September.

Top left: Aspens intermingle with evergreens for ever-changing scenery along the gravel road toward Boreas Pass. *Bottom left:* Looking down from the steep road, there is a view of the previous historic gold mining site of Hamilton.

Top right: Roberts Cabin, from the mid-1800s, was part of the railroad, and was used as a residence, a blacksmith's shop, and stables. *Bottom right:* The evening sun highlights a ridge and aspens along Boreas Pass Road. (Photos by Linda Nagy)

First snow

Above: The mountains, ridges and heights around Alma get their first snowfall as early as September, which adds to the beauty of South Park's fall. *Top right:* Colorful aspens stand out against snowy peaks. *Bottom right:* Ice is forming on the rivers in South Park.

A layer of ice covers the Middle Fork of the South Platte River at the historic Buffalo Peaks Ranch.

Winter, Serenity, Solitude and Wind

Morning sunlight gives a soft, warm glow to the snow-covered meadows in the Mosquito Range. Despite the high elevation, the Gray-crowned Rosy-Finch, forages for food.

"Every mile is two in winter."
-George Herbert

Forceful winds from the north strip fresh powdery snow off the trees in the Tumble Creek area.

Winter storms in the high country

Top left: Bristlecone pine trees disappear in whirling snow at Buckskin Gulch.
Top right: High winds blast the mountain peaks above Kite Lake Campground.
Bottom: A rancher comes to the rescue with feed for the cows at a ranch near Tarryall.

Facing page: Ground blizzards are part of the high country winter conditions in and near the town of Fairplay.

Blizzard!

"It is not the mountain we conquer, but ourselves".
- Sir Edmund Hillary

Snowshoeing, sledding and cross-country skiing are favorite outdoor activities at 11,542-foot-high Hoosier Pass. From the snow-covered and wind-blown meadows above the pass, one has excellent views of the Placer Valley toward the south and the Mosquito Range toward the west.

A lonely bristlecone pine stands high above the Sacramento Creek Valley.

Left: An immature bald eagle, perched on a fence post, ruffles its feathers on a warm winter afternoon along County Road 59. *Top right:* The hare's winter fur blends in with the snowy white surroundings beside Elkhorn Road. *Bottom right:* A mule deer stops grazing at the sight of onlookers near Guffey.

"The love for all living creatures is the most noble attribute of man."
- Charles Darwin

Inset: A jenny and her offspring keep a curious but watchful eye on the photographer. *Bottom:* This part of a growing herd of wild burros roams the prairie between Hartsel and Eleven Mile Reservoir.

Buffalo return home from the range near Hartsel.

Left: Looking for food after a snowstorm, a small herd of pronghorn climbs a hill at dusk. *Above right:* A pronghorn buck poses for a portrait.

Heavy, snow-laden lodgepole pines stand tall, like sentinels, beside County Road 12 near Park City.

South Park's own Devils Tower, the Eagle Rock, is a prominent landmark that is seen from County Road 77, also known as the Tarryall Road.

From the upper ridge of Kenosha Pass, the vast beauty of the snow-covered plains and surrounding mountain ridges of South Park appear much as they did to the newcomers more than a century ago.

Elevenmile Canyon

From the Spillway Campground, a moderate hiking trail (left) leads to Outlook Rock. It gives the hiker a spectacular view of frozen Eleven Mile Reservoir (center), a popular ice-fishing destination. Even in the wintertime, Elevenmile Canyon (right) is a great place to visit.

113

On a cold winter day, the setting sun gives a reddish cast to
South Park City log buildings and to Red Hill in the distance.

Withstanding harsh winters

Above: Rough-hewn log structures, such as a blacksmith's cabin and a former stagecoach building, which was moved from Mosquito Pass to South Park City, have endured long, harsh winters. Imagine how their hardworking occupants lived over a century ago. *Left:* An old bunk house still stands at the historic Tarryall Ranch along U.S. 285.

The bright morning sun's glow makes this snow-covered rancher's
wagon and young pine tree part of an idyllic winter scene.

Guffey's winter street scene

Like a picture from the past, Guffey, in the southeastern corner of South Park, reflects both the spirit and appearance of a turn-of-the-century town. Strolling across the snowy street is Guffey's unofficial mayor, a black cat named Monster.

The snow-covered Mosquito Range appears like a glowing jewel in the light of the rising morning sun.

South Park's Best Wildflower and Fall Color Hikes/Drives

1 Upper Buckskin Gulch, County Road 8,
Kite Lake, Emma Lake, South Park Fourteeners
drive, hike Wildflowers
2 Loveland Mountain, CR 8, FR 450/451,
four-wheel drive, hike Wildflowers
3 Upper Mosquito Gulch, CR 12, FR 696,
four-wheel drive, hike Wildflowers, Fall Color
4 Valley of the Sun, Sacramento Creek, CR 14,
drive, hike Wildflowers
5 Upper Fourmile Creek, Mt. Sherman CR 18,
Horseshoe Mountain, Forest Road 603
drive, four-wheel drive, hike, bike Wildflowers
6 Weston Pass Road, CR 5/22, Rich Creek Trail,
drive, hike Wildflowers, Fall Color
7 Lower Buffalo Meadows, Lynch Creek Trail,
FR 431/FR 43, drive, hike Wildflowers, Fall Color
8 Beaver Creek Meadows, FR 659, Mt. Silverheels
four-wheel drive, hike Wildflowers
9 Como, Boreas Pass, County Road 33,
drive, hike, bike Wildflowers, Fall Color
10 Jefferson Lake Trail, County Road 35/37,
drive, hike Wildflowers, Fall Color
11 Colorado Trail, both sides of Kenosha Pass,
hike Wildflowers, Fall Color
12 Lost Creek area, County Road 56,
drive, trail system, hike Wildflowers, Fall Color
13 Tarryall Valley, Tarryall Reservoir, CR 77,
drive Wildflowers, Fall Color
14 LaSalle Pass, Forest Road 44,
four-wheel drive Wildflowers
15 Elevenmile Canyon, County Road 96,
drive, hike Wildflowers
16 Eleven Mile State Park
trail system, hike Wildflowers
17 Thirtynine Mile Mountain, CR 116, FR 270,
high-clearance vehicle, drive Wildflowers
18 Black Mountain area, CR 88, FR 108/107,
drive Wildflowers, Fall Color
19 Dicks Peak, CR 108, FR 261,
high-clearance vehicle, drive Fall Color
20 Eleven Mile Reservoir to Guffey, CR 59/102,
drive Wildflowers, Fall Color
21 High Creek Fen off U. S. 285,
drive, walk Wildflowers
22 Jefferson, County Road 34,
drive Wildflowers
23 Sheep Valley, Twelvemile lake, FR 426/176/175/173,
four-wheel drive, Wildflowers, Fall Color
24 Fourmile Creek, CR 18 Limber Pine Trail,
drive, hike, Ancient limber pine grove
25 Buckskin Gulch, CR 8, FR 448/787, Windy Ridge,
drive, four-wheel drive, hike, Ancient bristlecone pines

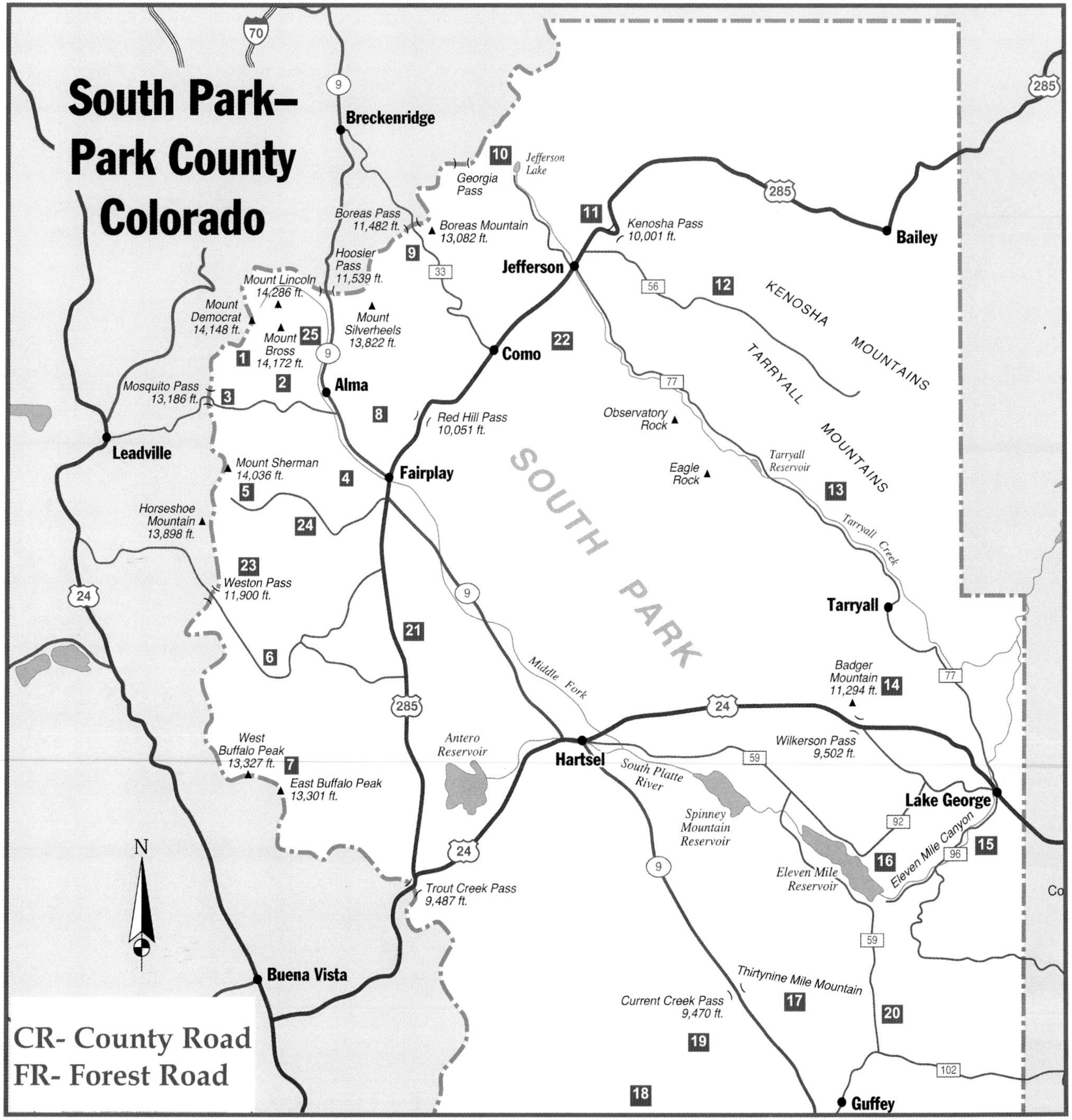

South Park–
Park County
Colorado
CR- County Road
FR- Forest Road
N
Breckenridge
Leadville
Alma
Fairplay
Como
Jefferson
Bailey
Tarryall
Hartsel
Lake George
Buena Vista
Guffey
SOUTH PARK
KENOSHA MOUNTAINS
TARRYALL MOUNTAINS
Mount Lincoln 14,286 ft.
Mount Democrat 14,148 ft.
Mount Bross 14,172 ft.
Mount Silverheels 13,822 ft.
Hoosier Pass 11,539 ft.
Boreas Pass 11,482 ft.
Boreas Mountain 13,082 ft.
Georgia Pass
Jefferson Lake
Kenosha Pass 10,001 ft.
Mosquito Pass 13,186 ft.
Red Hill Pass 10,051 ft.
Mount Sherman 14,036 ft.
Horseshoe Mountain 13,898 ft.
Weston Pass 11,900 ft.
West Buffalo Peak 13,327 ft.
East Buffalo Peak 13,301 ft.
Trout Creek Pass 9,487 ft.
Observatory Rock
Eagle Rock
Tarryall Reservoir
Tarryall Creek
Badger Mountain 11,294 ft.
Wilkerson Pass 9,502 ft.
Middle Fork
Antero Reservoir
South Platte River
Spinney Mountain Reservoir
Eleven Mile Reservoir
Eleven Mile Canyon
Thirtynine Mile Mountain
Current Creek Pass 9,470 ft.

Spectacular sunsets occur year-round in South Park's high country.